THE LAST ORGASM

Nin Andrews

Also by Nin Andrews

Miss August
Our Lady of the Orgasm
Why God is a Woman
The Circus of Lost Dreams
The Secret Life of Mannequins
Southern Comfort
Dear Professor
Sleeping with Houdini
Midlife Crisis with Dick and Jane
Any Kind of Excuse
Someone Wants to Steal My Name (editor)
The Book of Orgasms and Other Tales
Why They Grow Wings
Spontaneous Breasts
The Book of Orgasms

THE LAST ORGASM

Nin Andrews

Etruscan Press

Etruscan Press
Wilkes University
84 West South Street
Wilkes-Barre, PA 18766
(570) 408-4546

www.etruscanpress.org

Published 2020 by Etruscan Press
Printed in the United States of America
Cover image: *Red Ball* © Michael Bergt
Cover design by Carey Schwartzburt
Interior design and typesetting by Aaron Petrovich
The text of this book is set in Whitman.

First Edition

17 18 19 20 5 4 3 2 1

Library of Congress Cataloguing-in-Publication Data

Names: Andrews, Nin, author.
Title: The last orgasm / by Nin Andrews.
Description: Wilkes-Barre, PA: Etruscan Press, 2020.
Identifiers: LCCN 2019013637 | ISBN 9781733674119 (paperback)
Classification: LCC PS3551.N444 A6 2020 | DDC 811/.54--dc23
LC record available at https://lccn.loc.gov/2019013637

Please turn to the back of this book for a list of the sustaining funders of
Etruscan Press.

This book is printed on recycled, acid-free paper.

For Jim, first, last, and always

All of the orgasm's problems stem from her inability to sit quietly in a room alone.

—Blaise Pascal

The Last Orgasm

Contents

Part 2: Truth According to Nin

Part 3: Nin and I

Part 4: The Last Orgasm

Acknowledgments

Many thanks to Kathleen McGookey, Claire Bateman, Nancy Mitchell, Jeff Friedman, Philip Brady, and the editorial staff at Etruscan Press, whose insights, encouragement, and editorial assistance made this book possible.

Also, I would like to thank the editors of the following journals for publishing some of the poems in this collection, some in different forms and with different titles:

AGNI, The American Journal of Poetry, Coconut, Conduit, DMQ Review, Five Points, Gargoyle Magazine, Harpur Palate, jubilat, KYSO Flash, The Laurel Review, Mid-American Review, New Flash Fiction Review, PoetsArtists, Plume, River Styx, Scapegoat Review, Sentence, Triggerfish.

I would also like to thank the editors of the following anthologies for including poems from this collection:

New Micro: Exceptionally Short Fiction, edited by James Thomas and Robert Scotellaro, published by W.W. Norton & Co., 2018.

Misrepresented People: Poetic Responses to Trump's America, edited by Maria Isabel Alvarez and Dante Di Stefano, published by NYQ Books, 2018.

I'd like to thank Marc Vincenz and Danny Lawless of MadHat Press for publishing the chapbook *Our Lady of the Orgasm*, in which some of the poems previously appeared.

THE LAST ORGASM

Preface

If anyone reads this book, they will think they know what kind of person I am. They will, I am certain, imagine me as someone else, someone I can never be—simply because I have written this book of orgasms, and this book will do that to them, and to me. It will make me appear to be the kind of person who is in the position to write about orgasms, who knows all about orgasms: their songs and dances and secret languages. They might go so far as to compare me to Noah Webster, claiming that just as he compiled an entire opus of words, carefully defining and distinguishing each one's particular origin, pronunciation, spelling, and proper usage, so I have collected an opus of orgasms. And I will have to admit, with some surprise, that even if I don't imagine myself to be that sort of person, even if I don't consider myself an author anymore, much less an author of an opus of orgasms, even if I no longer converse with orgasms in my daily life, the orgasms continue to seek me out, as orgasms will, as if they need my blessing, as if I and only I can hear their pleas, their wishes, their last breaths.

PART 1

Truth According to the Orgasm

The orgasm has been contemplating the title,
The Last Orgasm

and she wants to tell you, dearest reader, that there is no such thing. She wants you to believe that she is immortal, that she is a nymph, a mermaid, a goddess or god, a saint, even Our Lady of the Orgasm, the one and only and everlasting . . .

And besides, she asks, who would write a book like this? Who can say when the last orgasm will be? Or if it has already passed?

The orgasm is afraid you have forgotten her

that you, like Nin, no longer feel her like a tingle, a tug, or a whispered word in the back of your mind. That you have taken from her whatever you wished, whatever you wanted, whatever you thought you must have. And you have tossed her aside without looking back.

It happened so easily, she sighs, as easily as pulling a thread from a hem—unraveling her slowly at first, then faster and faster. Now she wakes, late and alone, with a memory of all she has lost, all that once shaped the hours around her like a lit and shimmering gown.

The Orgasm Wants to be Famous

She thinks success could be her best revenge. It's not enough for her now, merely to be alive. To feel bliss in brief moments. No, she wants to be seen. Known. She wants everyone to cheer her on. And why shouldn't they? She knows she's a very special orgasm. She can see it every time she looks at her reflection, pirouetting before the mirror, then leaping this way and that. She cannot take her eyes off of herself. She is as lovely as a star. How could so few know she exists? She imagines the world fluttering around her like insects around a lamp. The image gives her pause. She thinks again. She selects a more appealing image. Perhaps they will flit around her like fireflies around the moon.

The orgasm decides to learn about social media

because that is where Nin says fame happens these days. And where the future lies. Even an orgasm has to keep up with the times. It's no longer satisfying simply to be an orgasm in red heels. She must also exist on the web. So she logs herself in. Soon she has Friends—so many Friends. And Likes. Oh, how she loves the Likes! Every day she yearns for more. More and more Likes. How many Likes, she wonders, equal one moment of bliss? The number rises and rises. Will she ever receive enough?

After a while, she begins to feel frivolous. A bit exposed. She worries that she lacks depth. Her encounters are too frequent, too fleeting. She fears she's becoming the kind of orgasm who merely tickles the surface of the lake. Who never dives deep like a fish, or flies high like an angel. How could she, when her legs are tucked beneath her, her wings folded neatly across her back? Outside, the clouds rush past like messages from another world. And the sky turns from blue to black.

The orgasm wants to open a Twitter account

but she isn't sure what to tweet. At first, she follows other tweeters. They tweet and tweet, forever singing of their wonderful selves. Even when she's sleeping, they're tweeting. Even when a snow-covered tree falls on a power line and cuts off her electricity. Even when she wakes the morning after, cold and shivering, and wraps herself in a robe. One day, she decides to tweet, too. "I am lighting up a cigarette," she tweets. "And I am telling you the one real truth." She licks her lips and smiles. "I am your last orgasm." She enjoys the silence that follows and is just about to sign off of Twitter forever. But then someone retweets her tweet. And someone else retweets the retweet. A little flutter begins in her heart. She sucks in deeply and glows like the tip of her cigarette.

The Orgasm Decides She Must Become a Brand

Otherwise, she will be like every other aspiring orgasm—i.e., anonymous. Lost among side streets and absent minds. But how can she become unique? How can she separate herself from the others? There are so many. She thinks of them with disdain, those everyday orgasms—so irksome, like used cars with their ignition problems, their lubrication issues, their broken distributors and failing circuitry. She's nothing like them. Of course she isn't. She's sleek and shiny and freshly painted. She decides she must become a niche orgasm, a brand all her own—something everyone desires but few ever possess, much less drive.

The orgasm is building a website

but is not sure what to put on her home page. She wants to draw something to fill the empty space. She imagines past admirers and ex-lovers stopping by, like you or Nin, wanting to know her every detail. "How is she?" they ask. "Has she aged? Has she grown fat and wrinkly and sad?" She knows they are watching her from afar, picturing her with their minds' eyes. Their presence makes her shudder. Makes her want to design the page as a cemetery or a cemetery as a page between her and the world. All it takes, she reminds herself, is a shovel and the knowledge of what to do with the dirt. (This, too, is part of social media, she reasons.) She draws a graveyard with maple trees and tombstones, an ex-lover's name on each one. She blesses them all as they once blessed her. She wishes them to rest in peace beneath a wintry wind and a mat of dry leaves.

The Orgasm Is Stumped by the About Me Page

After all, what does she have to say for herself? That she was once a cello? Well, not a cello exactly, but the notes that emerged? No, not the notes exactly, but the aura of the notes, the small ache they left in the sky like an imprint in blue—though it wasn't a sky exactly, but the cloudless space that opens and opens inside every woman. (She always did have a preference for women.)

The orgasm needs a photo of herself

preferably a headshot to go with a short bio. She takes a selfie leaning against a tree, looking too posed—not at all *au naturel* as she'd planned. She takes another selfie leaning on her silver Ford Mustang, smiling. Behind her, written on the window's condensation, is her message to the world. She throws them both away. Then she lets her hair cover her eyes and mouth and tries again. She doesn't want everyone to know what she looks like. No orgasm does. There is a rule against an orgasm who shows too much in public. A rule against an orgasm who shows too much in private—who lets just anyone gaze into her soft, blue soul.

One Evening, the Orgasm Decides to Give Up on Social Media

She no longer cares if she has any Friends. After all, the only question they ever ask is "How many orgasms can a man have?" It reminds her of that question, "How many angels can dance on a pinhead?" They never ask about her true nature or beliefs or dreams, her mood swings or dietary preferences, her favorite pastimes or films or dance steps. No questions about how she flew out of the body of God, singing and dancing and flaming as she fell.

The orgasm thinks people might prefer poodles

to orgasms. If orgasms were poodles, people could simply buy them at Pet World. Or keep them on leashes and show them off at the park. The best could perform at Madison Square Garden. Of course, the people would have to take good care of their orgasms—perhaps line their cages with flannel bedding and bathe them once a month with specialty soaps. (Few appreciate their natural scent—fish left out in the sun.) Some might think an occasional squirt of Febreze could fix them right up, but orgasms are sensitive to sprays and frequently suffer allergic reactions. No one wants to end up in an emergency room. Or worse, the morgue. Nor does anyone want to explain what happened, or who is to be blamed. *It's so sad*, the orgasm thinks. After all, orgasms offer such pleasure to humans; humans owe their orgasms at least the same care they give their beloved, pampered pets.

The orgasm grows sad

so very sad. How can she survive if everyone is staring at their computer screens instead of her? She thinks and thinks. Maybe she can become a poet or a painter. Maybe she can join an artist colony or take classes and give color and meaning to her life. She looks out the window at a goldfinch swooping across the meadow. She opens her windows, her doors, her mind. She steps outside and flaps her arms slowly, watching as the earth disappears beneath her feet.

The orgasm joins an artist colony

but instead of painting or writing, she becomes obsessed with a certain woman. She watches her all season long. The woman is Vietnamese, a poet, almost fifty. *What is it about her?* the orgasm wonders. After all, the poet is neither young nor beautiful. Perhaps it's how the poet moves with her thoughts, swaying slightly as if in a dream, that attracts her. How, when she stares at the ceiling, clouds pass through her, along with wind and summer rain. The more the orgasm watches, the more she wants the woman. She wants her the way the starving want bread with butter and a steaming pot of tea. She would ask her questions, too—if only she could form words on her tongue, like the poet. One night, when the woman is preparing for bed wearing nothing but a towel, her black hair spilling over her shoulders, she feels the orgasm's presence. She addresses her directly. "I think you have been watching me," she says. "I think you want to have me." She's that kind of woman. She speaks her mind. She knows the difference between one who lusts and one who loves. But then she adds, "I'm sorry, but I have lost my desire. It left with my lovers. I had three, but they abandoned me after I had a double mastectomy." Lifting her shirt before the mirror, she exposes the empty space where her breasts once hung. She expects the orgasm to turn away, to dissolve like mist as orgasms can. But instead the orgasm runs her airy fingers across the woman's chest, tracing her scars. She wonders if it's the suffering of humans that inspires their muse. "Such pain," she sighs as she caresses the woman's neck, her lips, her thighs. All night, she holds the woman, who weeps and weeps. The morning after, the woman feels as if she has bathed for the first time in years. A glow begins in her chest and belly and between her legs. She feels so calm yet alive, poems flow from her pen effortlessly, and sparrows fly to her window and sing as if she were one of them.

One day, the orgasm decides to move to Spain

to leave this country behind and reinvent herself in another landscape and language, but she can't figure out how to be an orgasm in Spanish. Her travel guide speaks only of *el orgasmo*. Do the Spanish not know *la orgasma*? And why not? After all, cats are both *el gato* and *la gata*, and they even have little *gatitos*, so shouldn't orgasms come in both genders? And have little *orgasmitos*?

Reading a little further, she wonders if an orgasm is simply *there* in Spain, as in: *Hay la orgasma*. No verb necessary. She likes that idea. The simplicity that she, the orgasm, could merely exist. She pictures a curtain opening to applause as she steps into the spotlight and takes a bow, her red hair sweeping the floor.

But then, she wonders, how did she get there? Was she had by another, as in English? *Tuvo una orgasma?* She's so tired of being had. Why can't she simply be? But what form of "to be" would she be? *Ser* or *estar?* She thinks *ser*. She tries it out as soon as she arrives in the airport in Madrid. "*Hola*," she announces, "*Yo soy la orgasma.*" The people turn away. Some break into a run, their suitcase wheels squealing behind them.

How lonely she feels then. Eavesdropping on passersby, she hears one say, "*Estoy muerto.*" In speaking of death, she realizes, one uses the verb *estar*. Death, it turns out, is an ongoing condition in Spain. If

19

death is ongoing, then surely the orgasm is, too—both of them being the all too familiar, uninvited guests in the backs of people's minds. Just thinking of this, the orgasm grows sad. "*Estoy triste*," she sighs. How lovely that sounds. *Triste*. Like a tree of stars.

The orgasm wants to write a memoir

so she can tell the world who she really is, but she doesn't know how to begin. When she thinks of the early days, she remembers how everyone warned her, "You'll never succeed. Many try to be orgasms but end up leading lives of quiet desperation." She knew she was different. In secret, she practiced. She told no one about this, not even her cat—and yes, all orgasms keep cats, which is why cats have little need of company. She began slowly, gathering her nerve. She only had one nerve, and it took everything she had to gather it up. Sometimes she gathered it for weeks at a time, starting at the ceiling, climbing first down the walls and then back up again, clinging for hours to the chandelier. Until, all at once, she would fall, twisting and turning in the air. She fell many times. Each time she rose again, a part of her became atoms of light, swirling up towards the sky. *This!* she thought each time. *This is it!* But it never was.

The orgasm decides to become a poet instead

and signs up for a class at a community college. She is happy to see they accept all kinds at the college. She doesn't feel a bit out of place. But her professor is forever berating the aspiring poets. "This is not a poem!" he tells the class. "You lack discipline. You lack form and style. Have you never read the classics?" The orgasm is reminded of her early days of learning how to be an orgasm. Often she'd heard, "That's no orgasm. Have you done your homework?"

There were so many tests back then, difficult tests. Walking through walls, for example. For real orgasms, everyone knows, there is no such thing as a wall. Nothing stops them. At first, she bumped into every wall she met, her skin a purple bruise. No matter how great her pain, she kept trying until she walked through wall after wall like a regular Houdini of orgasms. But when the walls moved through her, especially the stone ones, she caught a chill. Her temperature dropped twenty degrees, and she started to sneeze. It's like this, she learned, whenever you make love to the ones with no hearts or souls. She had only meant to walk through the walls, not love them. It was the same way with poems. She had to be careful which ones would travel inside her. And which she must never compose.

Write about yourself

the writing professor tells the orgasm. But who is that? The orgasm has no clue. The professor suggests she familiarize herself with dictionaries, and she does. She opens first the *English Dictionary of Orgasms*, then the French. She prefers the French. *Don't we all?* she thinks. Just looking at a word like *fenêtre*, she enters its moonlit attic, then curls up and purrs like a cat. She doesn't bother with the German orgasms—she has heard rumors that they are the ones who mistake the orgasm for a sneeze. Or is it vice versa? She's not sure. But she does want to make distinctions. She is an orgasm with taste.

But then she decides it doesn't really matter who she is. After all, the others in the class are simply describing their past, as if that defines them. So she describes the emptiness of her own childhood. The long, pale days in a remote town where even the schoolhouse had hollow rooms and classes full of hours that would never end. The orgasm was so small, no one noticed her or commented on her tiny pink hands. It was then that she began to long for something else. Anything else. Her longing grew. It made her ache and burn, traveling up and down her spine and the hairs on her legs like a flame. Until, one day, she shone like a small sun. Others began to look at her then. They sought her company again and again. Some thought of her as the only recess they ever had.

The Orgasm Fell in Love
with Her Writing Professor

"Every student did," the orgasm sighs. "I thought he liked me best. He said I was the most talented. But then he sliced me open, his words like fire ants traveling deep inside, making tunnels and nests. When there was nothing left for them to sting or bite, when I was but a filmy bride, a cloud, a fragment of moonlight, a single line, they left me. So did he.

"That, I have learned, is how poets are made."

The professor knew she needed help

so he kept her after class, long after the other students had left. One night he told her the story of Persephone. Maybe he thought she was so ignorant, she didn't know about the seasons, or how the world is ruled by sleazy gods. That it's a wonder anything blooms. Then he took out a pomegranate, cut it open with a pocketknife, and gave her a smug, lopsided grin. "What are you doing?" she asked as seeds leaked onto her white, white skin.

The orgasm reads a book of recipes

on self-healing, written by a priest. The first ingredient is silence.
She tries her best to hush. The second is a black cape. She covers
herself from head to toe in shame. The third, a magnifying glass, that
she may see herself and despair. She closes her eyes and falls asleep,
a wet rag over her forehead. Outside the window of her dream, a
woman is painting a flowering pear tree. With each brush stroke, the
tree fills with song and leaves. The orgasm rests on its limbs and lets
the wind fool with her flame-red hair.

Sometimes I feel so inspired

I think I am flying. Yes, flying far away. So far away, in fact, that between you and me and Nin, I am at a loss for words. *So this is what it's like to be an artist,* I think. Which brings me to the question: If I had to choose between being an orgasm and writing about one, which would it be?

"Oh Yellow Bird," I sigh as I gaze outside. "Oh Yellow Sun, Yellow Mood flooding my office with longing, I want to surrender to you. I want to give up all my bad habits."

I am so filled with bliss, I do not write. I cannot. "What should I do?" I ask Nin. She doesn't answer. So I watch her. And I do what Nin does.

Word by word, line by line, I change my mind. I change my mood, my laundry, my socks. I change the sun into wind, the wind into clouds and grief. I talk about my soul as if it were a shroud, my heart as if it were lost. Then I change it into a housefly, an egg, a frying pan.

Yes, I lie. Today, like Nin, I write lies.

If I were a poem

for Denise Duhamel and Maureen Seaton

I would want to be a sonnet composed
by my friends, Denise and Maureen. I can already
see myself in one of their whimsical scenes, but not
in their novelettes. No, I'd rather star in a comic
strip, a fable, or a fairy tale. Which? I'm not sure.
An insomniac, I'd make a lousy Sleeping Beauty.
Even drugs don't work on me. And my natural color
is pink, so I'm no Snow White. But I could be
Little Red Riding Hood, Goldilocks, or The Princess
and the Pea. I often pretend I'm just a sweet
dumb thing, but I always know whom or what
I've been sleeping with: a bear, a wolf, or tiny green peas
(though I call my peas *petits pois*, a French term
also used to describe Thumbelina's new breasts).

The Orgasm Writes a Short Biography of Nin

As a child, Nin played
alone. She hated birthdays,
Barbie, and the freckles on
her nose. Animals
were her best friends.
At night, she stayed awake
and spoke with ghosts.

When I first visited her,
she hid beneath the sheets,
ashamed.
She told friends
she'd never heard of me.
Even then, she lied.

Now here I am,
the author of her life.
Imagine that!

PART 2

Truth According to Nin

Last Night

Last night I dreamt
that the bees—the many golden bees
that hum inside my heart—
were leaving, one by one,
flying through a hole in the screen
and into the night.

In the morning, I could not think
or write. I took out
yesterday's poems and erased
them, one line at a time.
What terrible errors! I thought.
No use trying to make poetry
from my old failures.

There was no light
inside my words, no truth
to bring joy or tears to my eyes—

only the same lonely child
I have hated all my life.

Soul Mate

When I was a girl, I had a dirty soul. I hoped no one would notice. Sometimes I took it off and tried to clean it—to rinse it with a hose or put it in the washer. But the dirt wouldn't come off. Sometimes it dried to a fine gray dust and rose up my nose and gave me such a head cold, I couldn't stop sneezing. "Allergies," I said to anyone passing by. Other times, my soul refused to dry. If I put it in the dryer, the thing shrank like a wool sweater. If I hung it in the bathroom, it absorbed all the smells of the goings-on in there: urine, shit, hair sprays, toilet cleaners. But if I pinned it to the clothesline outside, the clouds gathered, and the rains followed. Sometimes there was even a monsoon. (Souls, they give you such trouble.) I'd end up rushing out to grab it before the rivers rose. Eventually, I gave up and put the soul back on, still damp and cold. What a terrible sensation, like clinging to a swamp. That's when my first lover came along. He was always telling me to hush—stop complaining, stop being such a perfectionist. He had a thing for troubled girls. He held me close, his fingers so hot, so impatient, so full of lust, they left imprints on my inner thighs. After we made love, I'd lie awake wanting to talk. "I can't go on like this," I said. But he wasn't listening. He was fast asleep, my soul wrapped around him like a filthy old coat.

The Banned Orgasm

In the town where I grew up, orgasms were against the law—especially for women. The women dressed in heavy black cloaks. On windy days they looked like dark sails on the streets. If they exposed a wisp of hair, an ankle, a sliver of wrist, they were sent away. Locked up. Sometimes their clitori were cut off. (Yes, clitori, the plural of clitoris. Every woman had two or three back then. If she was smart, she kept the extras for a rainy day.) "Why?" I asked, but no one would talk about it.

By the time I was twelve, I wanted an orgasm. "Just one," I said. I knew it was a bad idea. The women tried to convince me to behave. They explained the risks. Who knows what could happen to a girl like me? A girl whose hair floated free like a cloud? A girl who let the birds nest inside her blouse? "Besides," they said, "God never had an orgasm. Why should you? Do you dare to make him jealous?"

"Yes!" I whispered softly. "Yes! Yes! Yes!"

My Mother's Advice

When I was a girl, my mother taught me that virginity is sacred. Virginity is a present a girl must keep for her future spouse, a present only he should unwrap. "You must be careful," she explained. "You don't want a man to discover you've already taken off the bows, the ribbons, the gift tags. You don't want to give him something used or secondhand."

That was the first time I realized how tightly wrapped I was. How taped and bound with string. How I was already owned by a man I didn't know. At night, when Mother was asleep, I peeled back my layers, little by little. *Who's in there?* I wondered. *And what?* I was careful, so careful, I reasoned that I could always rewrap myself.

That was before the visions began. Before the orgasm first sang.

The Visions

When I was a girl, they were always there, waiting to be seen. How could I explain it? Others never saw them—those heavenly beings that were forever eating the sugar cubes at teatime and stealing sips of my parents' coffee or tea. They winked at me conspiratorially, knowing I would never tell.

When I was sixteen, I woke one night and saw Our Lady of the Orgasm singing. She was filled by notes so beautiful, I ascended with her, up and up like bubbles in a glass of champagne before breaking into tears and falling back to earth as a shower of rain. The next day, I had such a high fever, my mother placed bags of frozen peas on my forehead. She knew I was changed. For years after, I pretended I was as ignorant as my parents, who walked through their days like children in a game of pin the tail on the donkey. But whenever I closed my eyes, I saw Our Lady again, her bosoms as round and rosy as beatified peaches.

The Truth about Our Lady of the Orgasm

She is unique among orgasms. She is as different from the other members of her tribe as water is from sand, as honey is from Tabasco sauce.

I will never forget one summer evening when I was sleeping on the porch. Just as I was drifting off, she arrived in all her splendor, quivering and chattering with the angels. In heaven, the angels informed me, statuettes of her are placed on altars and dangle from rearview mirrors. Angels and gods are known to rub her for good luck before flying to the depths below. But alas, she often forgets her divine nature, as men and orgasms are wont to do, and wreaks havoc wherever she goes.

The Accidental Orgasm

1.

"Really, I never intended to have an orgasm," I explained to anyone who asked. "Believe me—she just showed up. I had no choice but to act like a dog, panting and wagging my tail."

2.

It's good to accept the orgasm, I thought. But I was never one to watch in the mirror. She deranged my face. I never looked as pretty as I'd have liked.

3.

I always expected to have time, but the orgasm was gone in a blink. "Don't think about it," I told myself. I thought about it.

4.

The orgasm was like a bird. If I tried to hold on, she flew away or broke into wild singing.

5.

Some days, I feared the orgasm was abandoning me. Maybe she had already flown south for winter. I wondered if she'd ever loved me. Or I, her.

The Orgasm and Me

In my spare time, I tried teaching the orgasm how to dress, how to dance, how to carry on a polite conversation. In short, how to become a civilized member of society. This was no small task. Not for me, not for her—as you might have guessed, given the orgasm's proclivities and short bursts of emotion, not to mention her instability and lack of interest in decency. I'm not a complete dolt. I did understand the challenge.

But you can't always know how few cards you hold, or so the saying goes. It began easily enough. She didn't object when I simply suggested we shop for clothes. That she could no longer gad about in the nude. I gave her a pair of my old sneakers and a housecoat so that we could visit the local dress shops. "But what does an orgasm wear?" she asked, blinking in wonder while fondling colorful gowns and stockings and shoes, as if she were imagining sinking into each one. She had a distinct love for reds and blues and could not keep her hands off camisoles or pantyhose. But she wouldn't touch any earthy colors, anything that reminded her of the days she felt cast off and alone. "Color," she said, "is so suggestive."

What I had not anticipated were the salesmen, dogs, and strangers who followed us everywhere we went. Soon I had to give up on shopping and begin the more important lesson: teaching her how to speak, or, to be specific, how to say *no, go away* and *get lost!* No matter what I tried, she always sounded like a drowning woman, gasping for breath. Her *no* sounded like a *yes*. Her *go away* like *come closer*. Her *get lost: Stay, please—just a little longer.*

I should have known I was getting nowhere when, in a moment of poor judgment, I asked her to dance. "Oh yes!" she said as she encircled my waist and twirled me around and around, my hair flying outward, my chest arched like a bow. Her enthusiasm stretched up towards the sky, higher and higher, always higher. (Orgasms, they say, can travel the distance between heaven and earth in a flash.) Meanwhile, strangers and devotees of all sizes and shapes gathered around and knelt on the ground, drool spilling from their lips. And I, suddenly so small in front of her, begged her to come back to me. I assured her I would never try to tame her again. What else could I do? I, a tiny woman, dwarfed by an orgasm.

Her

In the early days, she said her name was Sea Foam. She said her name was Wave Girl, Delicious, Myrtle, Grace. (None of these names were true.) She said her mother raised her in a sunless sea. She was washed ashore in a tsunami. Or was it a hurricane? A sudden summer rain? She was all alone, clothed in strands of sticky hair. For weeks, she took shelter in a cave. Or behind a dune. Or a sailor's unmarked grave. Sand and pebbles clung to her skin. She stayed alive, sucking periwinkles and sea urchins from their shells. Drinking the dregs of whiskey from grimy bottles, beer from crinkled cans, water from cracked gull eggs. She spoke only with the cormorants, sandpipers, crabs, terns. She was discovered by a man who swam inside her like a fish. A woman who taught her arithmetic, penmanship, grammar, and how to wash her grubby hands. "By a genie who gave me one wish. You." Nice pickup line, yes? That was years ago, back when I hated nature, wet lips, her slimy, piscatory scent. My first memory is of her singing for five days straight. All those *oohs* and *ahhs*, followed by a fever, a thirst, a fire torching everything I knew. Every word I said. I tried aspirin, opiates, logic, toweling her off. Screaming. Long, chilly baths. Skinny-dipping in the night. "Diving into the whole cosmic reservoir," as she put it. When I finally closed my eyes, I dreamt in whale songs. Bubbles rose from my lips. No matter how I tried, I could never utter her name.

The Three Orgasms

In the stories of old, there were always three orgasms. The first orgasm talked about the earth, and watched it. (But who needs mere talk? And watching?) The second one listened to the earth, bending close to hear the winds and the rains and all of mankind's complaints. (But who needs mere listening?) Then there was the third.

The third one neither talked nor listened before she drifted through the clouds, slowly descending until, at last, she landed with a soft *pfft*. It was always summer when she arrived. On a scorching day, she walked the sunbaked streets, the soles of her feet blistering, but she didn't notice. She explored the shops and bars and cafés and the white stone cottages. She rang doorbells and entered homes and apartments and people's hearts. When people reached to shake her hand or hugged her close, or later, when they took her to bed, strange sounds burst from her lips. (No, she didn't speak their language. Or they, hers.)

"What happened to her?" the second one asked. "Did she die?"

"Oh yes, she died. Again and again, she died," the first one said as he peered over the edge. But all he could see from above was her dress swaying on a rocking chair, empty-armed and weeping, a single gold button spinning on the stone floor.

The Shadow of the Orgasm

Sometimes I saw her, or thought I did. Was it only her shadow? The shadow of an orgasm? But what is that? A dream? A memory—of someone I loved, once upon a time? But then again, maybe I didn't see her at all. Nevertheless, I approached her gingerly. She slunk away like a cat. Orgasms do that. They never let you look in their eyes. They're afraid of you coming too close, too fast, pulling their tails or dunking them in cold water. "It's okay," I wanted to say. But usually, something welled up inside me. Tears, for example. And desire. Suddenly I'd want to run towards her, to scoop her up in my arms. But I stopped myself. Stood still as a stone, feigning disinterest. She stopped, too. I cooed softly. Let her approach, whiskers twitching. Just as I reached to stroke her, she bit me. Hard. Blood trickled down my arm.

"I'm sorry!" she apologized. "I thought you weren't real!" She began licking me with her hot, pink tongue.

The year I suffered from SAD

I no longer wanted an orgasm. I no longer wanted to get out of bed or shower or rush out into the evening, as she and I had so often done. "You must rise and shine," she said, but I didn't budge. I couldn't even begin to rise, much less shine. "What is the matter with you?" she asked as I looked at my reflection and asked the same question. I tried. Really, I did. But nothing worked.

After a while, winter set in. I was chilled to the bone. For days, I sat by the window, staring at the sky. She sat on the windowsill beside me. On sunny days, she dripped. "Don't look," she whispered. "I'm crying." But that's just how she prayed. For an orgasm, prayer is similar to melting in the same way sin is like falling in your sleep.

"Let me die. Let me die one more time," she said, her lips barely moving. Outside, the neighbors threw snowballs and shoveled their sidewalks, turning their backs to her and me, as if afraid to look at us. But one man glanced our way. There was always one Good Samaritan out there. He didn't know the danger he was in.

Remembering Our Ex

I sometimes ask the evening air, "Who are you now? And where?"
I think of the anguish we caused, the orgasm and I, those sleepless
nights when our ex sobbed after we left him alone and undressed. He
cried so much one night, he had to wring out the sheets the morning
after. For weeks he howled like a dog at the moon. He texted and
phoned so often, but we never answered his calls. But then, one
day, he saw me standing alone at the Café Loup. He was amazed at
how ordinary I looked in my faded jeans, my tall black boots, smoke
billowing from my wind-chapped lips. That's when he asked, "Who
were you that made me pine for so long?" He never knew the truth.

Spiritual Advice from the Orgasm

"You must learn to concentrate," she said. "Keep your mind in the present." Of course, the orgasm is always present. But I lingered in the past. Often, I had fantasies. My favorites: a fire-eater, his head bent back, closing his lips around a blaze. A long-legged girl dressed only in a wedding veil, twirling faster and faster. (She had the loveliest long, skinny legs.) A bearded waiter asking what I wanted—he said he was only there to serve. The last time I saw him, I asked for a single glass of water. I was trying out abstinence, the primary ingredient in holiness. The second ingredient: a shaved head. Outside, the snow began to fall. I shivered, imagining myself a bald nun walking inside an ice cube.

One day, I performed a healing ceremony

where I walked on coals. Of course, I waited until the coals had cooled, then ran across them as fast as I could. But I tripped and fell, and the hem of my skirt caught fire. I rolled on the ground until I was nothing but smoldering shame. Afterwards, I worried. What if the fire had spread? What if it had lit up my loose threads, traveled across the grass and into the forest and the town beyond? What if it had become a flaming torch, or I had? A torch that set the world ablaze? I couldn't stop thinking about it. *From now on, I must live alone*, I thought as I cried myself to sleep. My dreams turned to flames and burned a thousand pinholes in the night.

The orgasm convinced me I need her after all

even if it's true she did not exist
until I slipped beneath the ocean
and, like the drowning,
tried to cling to the sky,
to the eleven stars I counted
(I always counted back then),
to the limbs of wet black trees
and the bulging yellow moon,
and, when crying out, I begged,
"Please, please, oh please,
let me die!"
And she did.

PART 3

Nin and I

Other People's Orgasms

I am trying to sleep beside Nin, but she is wide awake in this roadside motel in Poland, Ohio, smelling of new carpet and cigarettes. It's late. Midnight, one o'clock, two . . . Nin hears the door to the next room open and slam shut. A couple starts giggling, then talking softly. They start having orgasms. Loud, celebratory orgasms. "Oh, oh, oh!" they scream. Nin closes her eyes and enters their room, their bed, their orgasms. Then she, too, falls fast asleep.

The Bad Orgasm

What a troubling thing it is. Nin brings it along wherever she goes. There in her luggage, her purse, the back of her mind. She keeps going over and over it, like a poem she can never finish or get right. But she never gives up. After a while, it becomes so familiar. Like a best friend or a dog, the kind that never leaves your side. That keeps licking and licking. And barks from time to time.

The Orgasm Guard

He is with Nin always and everywhere. He is as buff as a bull and as old as a Greek god, and so wise. He has to be. For he is the orgasm guard. The one who knows what stirs beneath her skin and mind. Who sees what lovers come and go, long before or after they leave. He protects her from the obsessive ones, the sinister ones. Even the ones who hate her, who blame and curse her, their cold, smokers' fingers reaching out for her again and again. Oh yes, it's so! Hate is as seductive as love—this is what every orgasm guard knows.

The Red Ball

I am standing on my head at dawn, a red ball balanced on my feet, when Nin walks in. "What are you doing?" she asks.

"Can't you see? I'm balancing the world on my feet," I say. "Wanna try?" I can tell she wants to. She wants to take the world in her hands and feel it spin. But she pauses. "I have to pee," she says in a mournful tone. "Back in a minute." In less than a minute, the world, all red and glowing, is gone. So am I.

This happens again and again. I don't know how many worlds have been lost while Nin is in the bathroom.

The Frozen Orgasms

I keep telling Nin—she should not dwell on these last years, when we lie apart at night and stare at the ceiling, trying not to ask how we became two cold shapes in the freezer department of our lives.

No, we should think only of those early days, when we were both as shiny and new as green peas. Only slipperier.

Her Secret

Everyone knows that Nin has a secret—a secret she must never tell. She can't. She can't even tell her therapist or closest friends. Not even when she grows older, not even when her hair turns white and her mind misty. *Do others feel this way?* she wonders. Even as a girl, she knew how to lie. How to hold back that part of herself she most wanted to give away—to develop the art of not telling. The gift of not giving. Now, even if you chopped off her arms, her legs, her beautiful red hair, she wouldn't say a word. No storyteller worth her salt would tell. Instead, she will make up another story.

Nin and I

The other one, the one called Nin, is the one things happen to. *Here I am*, I want to shout, but these days she is indifferent to my presence. When I ask if there is anything I can do for her, she stands there, gazing out the window. That's when I feel so empty. So lost. Invaded by sadness. Days go by, and no one enters her mind. Least of all me.

She, of course, goes about her business, sipping her rosehip tea, writing her poems, sleeping late wrapped in a cocoon of sheets. (What a sloth she's become!) She's just an example of an ordinary American woman with dishwater blonde hair, an absent mind, and too many freckles. But I never tire of her, though I always protest when seen as an object. "Trying to have one," she sighs. As if I were just one. And require great effort.

Sometimes when I can't sleep, I stare at her, wondering what it's like to sleep inside flesh, much less to dream. I want to sink deep in her skin and see if something is still there, just for me, or if she will cry out. Isn't that what we all want? A little pain and rage, mixed with bliss? A little sugar with our sorrow? Just to know we're really here? She must have heard my thoughts, felt them, or sensed them passing like clouds overhead, because last night, for no apparent reason, she left all at once. There was no drama, no excuse-making, no fight. She simply packed her things, walked outside, closed the door, and turned the key.

After she was gone, a single wasp flew through a hole in the screen and circled the room before banging into a lamp, trying to enter the bulb. I found a note on the desk in her tall, loopy script: "I have never felt so alone." I wasn't sure if she meant she felt alone when she was with me, or after. Or if she has always felt that way. Or if it was I who taught her how alone feels.

I'm a Depressed Orgasm

I've been so blue lately, I've become just a faint memory of who I once was. I can't be the best company anymore. Not for you, not for anyone. But would you stay a while anyhow? Hold me? Or introduce me to your friends? Then maybe I could move on. I, who live alone in the dark, now that Nin is gone. But I can still delight. I promise. I have a few different moves and songs and tones of voice, some you have never heard. All I want is another chance. To be kissed, to be caressed. It feels so futile, though. When all I do these days is give birth to myself. No one wants that. Or just that. I miss it so. I miss a social life, you understand? Perhaps you have gone through something like this yourself? What? I've made you sad? You're crying? Now there are two of us. Let me hug you. Tight. A little tighter. Tighter! Ah, yes. What fun!

Advice from the Orgasm

When courting a man with a defect like, say, a tiny head, simply say, "Why, what a pinhead you are!" Say it as if you're admiring him. Don't lie or give him a line like, "You're not so small." Or, "I've seen heads tinier than that." Don't suggest he cover it up by commenting, "Well, now, shouldn't we find you a suitable hat?" There's no need to flatter him, comparing him to a king or an emperor. After all, everyone knows the story of Napoleon. How his head was so small, hats were forever slipping from his head. That's why he wore another hat beneath his hat. And another hat beneath his other hat, each snugger than the one before. His first wife, Joséphine, had to peel his head like an onion, one tight woolly hat after another, the poor thing. No wonder they had no heirs! But it was his second wife, Marie Louise, who removed his final chapeau. What a struggle it was! A dab of petroleum jelly might have helped, but that was fifty years before the birth of Vaseline. Scholars make a big deal out of this. They say that the very essence of Napoleon had slept under his cap for so long, it no longer dwelt in his wee head alone. Of course, any woman would have known that.

The Letter I Should Have Written to a Young Nin

Back in the beginning, in what I call the golden days, Nin used to ask if she was good—forever comparing our evenings together with others, fretting about her inadequacies, questioning if she should have said this and done that or kissed there. She asked and asked, as I fear she might have asked countless others before me. I should have begged her to give it up. I should have told her to ask herself, "Is this what you were meant to be? To do? Really? If not, do us all a favor: Give it up. But, if the answer is yes, and still yes, then please, learn a little silence." (I never cared for those chatty types who keep me up all night. Nor do I like those singing or moaning lovers who make me feel as if I'm sleeping in an aviary or a haunted house.) "And learn patience, why don't you? For isn't the beginning the most memorable? Those moments rife with anticipation? With your hair unclasped, spilling over your freckled shoulders, a blush just beginning like a warm wave washing over your breasts? And must you always complain when I am not there? Or not there yet? For what meaning would our lives, so full of yearning, have if what we wished for most were always close at hand? Or worse, already and easily in our sweaty grasp?"

Not Having an Orgasm

It's too hot tonight. So hot, I can feel Nin not having an orgasm again. She's sweating profusely, feeling slightly smelly, and she keeps worrying about the book she's writing on orgasms. (God, the woman worries too much!) She worries, *What if nobody reads it?* She worries, *What will they think if they do?* She thinks maybe she should give up writing, go back to school, become a banker, a professor, a lawyer, yes—one of those slick Manhattan types in black suits and heels, the kind she meets at cocktail parties who ask what she does, and when she says "I write poetry" in that high-pitched, apologetic voice that makes me want to slap her, they smile politely and ask, "About what?" Before she can answer, they've turned away, and she blushes with anger, the color rising up her neck. But there's this one guy who overhears and starts watching her. He's smoking a cigarette and drinking a martini when he taps her arm and asks, "Don't I recognize you? You know, I love poetry, too."

The way he looks at her gives me the creeps. Nin feels suddenly claustrophobic and steps outside for a breath of air, but he follows, says he's interested in her poems—in fact, he's a poet, too. "Wanna see my sestina?" he asks. She smiles politely and nods, even though there's an unpleasant glint in his eyes, and he's weaving, clearly drunk. "I gotta go now," she says, but he walks her to the door, then leans in close and squeezes her ass. "Baby," he whispers, "I could help you out. I know a man who'd publish a woman like you. Here's my number." And, just for a second, she believes him. She thinks, *Maybe it's not that hot after all*. That's when I hiss, "Maybe we should leave. Now! Go home. Run an ice-cold bath." And she does. (Poets, they're like that, yes? You never know what they'll do when desperation hits.)

The Golden Nugget

The Golden Nugget, for those who don't know, is a small, golden rocket ship that a woman can insert inside herself. And, according to the manual, that Golden Nugget will find places in a woman no man has been before. It will go on tour. Or what the advertisement calls "The Golden Tour."

Did you know there are entire galaxies in there, the directions claim, *complete with glittering stars and balmy planets and meteor showers?*

But there are warnings. After a while, some women grow afraid they are being taken over by the Golden Nugget. *What if the Golden Nugget is some kind of alien?* one lady worries. *What if one of those spaceships that landed ages ago in Roswell, New Mexico, brought aliens who found a secret way to impregnate women? They packaged themselves in plastic wrap and now wait on the shelves in sex shops across America. Unwitting women pop them inside, thinking they're just another dildo.* She thinks a lot of men wouldn't mind being mistaken for a dildo, but only the aliens would figure out how to do it.

But why worry now? she reasons as she sashays into the horizon, sighing with every step and at every bee and butterfly flickering past, and every drop of unpredicted rain.

What I Keep Telling Nin

You don't have to be good.
You don't have to get down on your knees
or apologize, or blame your ex.
You don't have to bring your new lover Hallmark cards
or chocolates, but an occasional bottle of Chianti
would be nice. You don't even have to let your
soft animal body love his hard animal body
more than once a week. (He has you penciled
in for Friday, 10:00 p.m., his place.
He'll order pizza. You might want to pick the DVD.)

And you don't have to listen when he tells you about his day
again, his long and tiresome day with his teenage daughter,
Brittany, who calls but hangs up when he offers advice,
or his secretary who has a habit of plucking
out her eyebrows, one by one, as she tells him
about her inability to lose weight, or his clients
who want legal advice on bankruptcy law—how best
to avoid responsibility for their company's toxic waste—
and how he still dreams of becoming the head
of his firm or a politician or a CEO,

and you don't need to talk about your day: how the sun
slid across the sky. How no words came to your mind

or the blank white page, and how empty you felt then,
how you took a nap in the lavender sheets
he gave you for Christmas, or how you walked the dogs
at dusk and a flock of geese flew overhead,
then landed in the tall grass by the path.
You tried to chase them away, but they rushed
at you, honking and hissing. And you thought, all at once,
that whoever you are, no matter how accomplished
or sad, the world rushes back at you
like these wild geese, and shits all over the place.

The Curse of the Orgasm

You might think by now that I would be used to it. After all, I've seen the annual crop of young lovers pull off the highway in Poland, Ohio, and step over the barbed wire fences to lay their blankets in the empty pastures. I have watched them closely, their eyes lit with anguish and desire as they gasp for breath. I have grazed freely on their nude skin, there beneath the willow trees.

But when all is said and done, when the lovers return to their clothes, their minds, their cars and homes, they slough me off and leave me outside like a Peeping Tom to peer through their windows at what was so briefly mine: the slender legs, the bent swan necks, the tender flesh of inner arms. And I realize how alone I am. How I have no soul to call my own, no body to break open again and again, or to shuck off like a husk of corn. "There is no such thing as a blessing," I sob as my mind darkens with twilight, and the wind sweeps softly through the grass.

If

If I see you again in the window, if I reach out and caress the red flame of your hair, everything that exists will vanish, little by little.

The sky will have no birds; the trees, no roots; the sea, no islands; time, no hours, no minutes, no seconds; the clock, no arms—only the blank face of a long-forgotten god gazing down at us.

There will be no winter, no spring, no summer—only a day like today with leaves drifting like windblown boats across a metallic sky

as the autumn rain extinguishes the fire in you, in me, and washes the implacable sadness from our lips.

Song of the Orgasm

Every atom belonging to me belongs to you, and you know it—you who loaf so freely about my soul and have for eons, you, as lean as a spear of meadow grass, a stalk of wheat, always I see you, and everywhere,

even here, when you are a thousand miles away, I can't help but breathe you in, your scent in every room in me, in every corner and shelf and dust mote, in every moment I inhale you, intoxicant that you are, illegal substance, I should not let you, not now, not ever, not you,

who are on my lips, tongue, fingers, hair, forever I taste the salt of you, the sorrows and song of you whom I am so in love with, I will go to the brink of my mind, exposed, nude, mad to be in contact with you.

In the Supermarket of Orgasms

What thoughts I have of you tonight as I walk the suburban sidewalks of Poland, Ohio, under the flickering streetlights with an ache in my bones and a loneliness brought on by my persistent solitude, a full moon, and a longing for you, love, yes you, whom I picture again and again in all your lovely shapes and sizes and flavors

as if I were walking the lit aisles of a supermarket of desire, selecting orgasms for every occasion with you, orgasms as ripe and red as these heirloom tomatoes, as illegal as dark chocolate, as ordinary and soft as a loaf of Schwebel's bread, and some so crisp, so green, that, like new fruit, they must be eaten under a full moon on a night like this

when I look up at the sky and see not the stars but a thousand faces of you, a thousand shapes of you, each so nude, so bright, I sob out loud until the leaves sing in the wind, and the dogs howl, and the dust cries out beneath my bare feet.

Black Dress on a White Carpet

You will leave me in Toledo, on a snowy day in winter, a day I already remember. You will leave me in Toledo—I already see you, stepping outside in your skimpy black dress, your tall boots, the wind lifting your hair. You don't look up or back—you are but an exclamation mark on a white page on a Sunday in winter in Toledo, Ohio. I know this because today is a Sunday, the church bells are ringing, the faithful in their fur coats and hats, hands buried deep in their pockets, are on their way to worship even as I write these lines, and I feel not you but the absence of you like a pearly winter glow even as I make love to you, even as I worship your lips, your thighs, your clavicle and hip bones and long slender toes, even as you fall asleep beside me, even as you call out my name in a dream, as your black dress sways on the wicker chair above the white carpet, and I see you as a dream in a black dress, an ache in my skin and deep in my bones, and suddenly I know you are leaving, and I will watch you leave. I have never felt so alone, so lost—I want to wake you, I want to tell you, "Love will tie us in knots, love will beat us with sticks, love will say he did nothing to us—you know how love is, so full of lies," but it will be too late, it already is, you are already leaving me, stepping outside, into the snow with no one but the sky as your witness, the winter birds, the trees, the wind.

A Simple Fact That Few Really Know

The orgasm can be either male or female. In daydreams, as in life, an orgasm switches genders as easily as man changes his jacket and pants, slipping one day into the life of a ballerina, spinning elegant pirouettes, and another into the cockpit of a pilot whose jet, even now, is gliding above the clouds. One might even become a deer fleeing from a coyote, or the coyote in hot pursuit. But no matter who or what she becomes, she is always a stranger here in this world. She can never feel the dirt beneath her feet any more than we can feel the sky caressing her hair as she rises. No matter how often she tries, she can never find a place or person to call her own.

The Orgasm and the Magic Maid

Opening his eyes one morning, the orgasm was alarmed to see that he had been transformed into a man. *Clearly, some terrible mistake has been made,* he thought, looking with horror at the dome of his belly and, worse, what hung between his thighs. "How hideous," the orgasm cried out, and then he went back to sleep.

Soon a woman began to shake him. "Look at you!" she shouted. "Sleeping all day! Why don't you get up and make something of yourself?" He didn't answer, but when she bent down to slip her stockinged feet into a pair of red pumps, displaying the slope of her hips, he felt a sudden urge to do what she said. But when he reached out to give her buttocks a mischievous squeeze and saw his hairy hand, he put it away immediately. All those brown spots on his manly hand! All those blue veins!

"What has happened to me?" he asked. "Perhaps this is just a nightmare." He closed his eyes, lay as still as a statue, and tried to fall back asleep.

A while later, he heard birds singing through an open window. A soft, warm light filled his room, and he tossed off the blankets and lay nude on top of the sheets. He felt a brief moment of peace and thought how life as a man might be okay after all. But then he heard a key in the door. Not long after, a loud *brrrring* filled the apartment. Before he could get out of bed, a woman wearing an apron and a little white cap with the words *Magic Maids* embroidered in red script across the front entered his room, pushing an Electrolux vacuum cleaner. *What's a Magic Maid?* the orgasm wondered.

Seeing the orgasm, the Magic Maid stopped what she was doing. "What kind of woman would leave *you* sleeping on her bed?" she asked, looking at him hungrily. The orgasm flinched beneath her eager gaze, and in spite of himself, a blush spread across his skin, and his penis began to bob upwards. "I wouldn't mind having a little piece of you myself," she grinned. And with that, she slid in beside him, the smell of Lysol filling his nostrils.

"I'm very tired," the orgasm said apologetically, but the Magic Maid didn't seem to hear him. "I have a headache," he added as she unbuttoned her blouse. "Would you mind taking a swig of Scope?" She didn't answer. Instead, she pressed her lips to his. "I would so love a cup of water," the orgasm added as politely as he could when he broke free for a moment. But the Magic Maid grabbed him in her firm hands and inserted her tongue in his mouth. "I'd rather not do this," the orgasm continued when he could speak again, but the Magic Maid ignored his every plea and blanketed him with her ample flesh, pressing all of him into her with gusto.

"Help!" the orgasm cried out as he felt his power waning away. The light of his soul flickered and dimmed into the Magic Maid. His last memory was the voice of what he thought was a pedestrian outside, or maybe someone calling a dog or a child or a god, he wasn't sure which. He only knew that the voice sounded desperate, that whatever was lost would never be found.

The Orgasm Blues

Sometimes an orgasm gets the blues and has to visit a shrink. What else can he do? He is aging. He has no defenses left, no ability to stay. Wherever he sits, there's a TV overhead showing the latest war, earthquakes, typhoons, mass shootings, diet plans, ads. All those ads! He can't look away. He stares at the images of Nike, detergent, Cialis, life insurance, Oreos, Budweiser, pizza, shiny lips. There were years, he remembers, when Nin wanted everything, her shopping bags filled to bursting. That was back when life was a green light, her body, a shiny red car, complete with that new car smell, and engines that revved and revved while her heart, like a child, pounded its tiny fists, screaming, "More! More! More!" Now he lies back on a leather couch as the clock arms sweep slowly past five minutes, ten minutes, fifteen. He is silent at first, and then he sobs and sobs, but he cannot speak. The therapist tells him to breathe, "Just breathe." Then asks what troubles his soul. "What soul?" he asks, his face a blank. There are no words to describe what is sleeping in his mind.

PART 4

The Last Orgasm

Orgasm

My husband was in bed, reading the news.
When I bent to kiss him, he said,
"Lie down, why don't you?" And
I did. "You're still reading the news," I said.

"Yes," he said, and absently
patted my arm. "What's happening?"
I asked. "Bibi Netanyahu just won
the election," he said.
That's when I had to leave.
I don't care for Bibi Netanyahu.
Neither does my husband.

I felt so lonesome then, so bereft.
I walked to the desk and began to type.
Words undulated in slow waves
through my mind. They did not tell
the truth. They said I live by the ocean
in a city of dust and crows. I'm the most
beautiful redhead alive. Today, wearing a green
satin blouse, I stretched out beneath the palm
trees to warm my nut-brown thighs.

I stopped writing. Outside, it was beginning to rain.
I sipped weak coffee and gave the dog
a biscuit. I called the poem "Orgasm,"
even if there was not a single orgasm
in that dusty seaside town.

The Innocent Lives of Orgasms

Tonight I am thinking of the innocent lives
of orgasms, of how they know
they will die
but not exactly how.
Like prisoners of war
before a firing squad,
I imagine them lining up happily
for their end.

How different they are
from the man and the woman
on this night when snow is falling
on the sleeping town of Poland, Ohio,
and an icy wind seeps under their doors,
and through their many cracks.

The woman—namely me—cannot sleep.
She gets up to riffle the pages of a book
she is writing, knowing there used to be
so much time to decide
what would happen next.
There used to be whole lifetimes ahead
for the man and the woman to live on and on
in her imagination, like the king

and queen of an interior countryside,
waging occasional wars, carrying away the wounded.

But now even warfare has come to a close.
They are peaceful, happy even, except
for a presence so difficult to define
of what could be the last lovely orgasm, there
in her margins, lettering its way onto the pages
and letting her know, as only an orgasm can,
that she shouldn't worry—the end will come
when it does, and then it will pass,
and then it will come again.

The Last Orgasm

What you have long suspected is true. I know. It happened to me on August 11, 2013, a Sunday. My husband served me coffee and croissants in bed. Ada, the terrier, joined us and snuggled beneath the covers. My husband placed a red cushion behind his head and read the *Times*. I turned on NPR. Krista Tippett was interviewing a Zen master on the program *On Being*. The Zen master said that all I needed was to follow my breath. So I tried following my breath. Until my breath became a sigh. That's when our visitor stopped in. She looked at me and then away and then apologized, "We've had a nice life together. We've seen a lot of sunsets. We've swum the length of three oceans. We've surfed the days, the months, the decades. I once held my breath for seven days just waiting for you to arrive. I've been ashore 3,141,592 times. And now I'm tired. Dog-tired, as you say."

Outside, a robin was singing. My husband listened and said nothing. He stood up and put on a terry cloth bathrobe. He looked out the window at what had once been the sea. We both did. We remembered years when the waves came up to the door. We thought they would keep rising and rising, crashing against our shoulders. We thought they'd wash us away. Now there was only sand. Miles and miles of sun-bleached sand.

"It's okay," my husband said. "I, too, am old. I am tired of fooling around." He picked up a broom and began to sweep. The sand was everywhere, blowing through the windows and beneath our doors. A single shell lay on the floor. He picked it up and gave it to me like an offering. "Something to remember me by," he said. When I pressed the shell to my ear, I heard the wind rushing through my empty rooms. I heard a tiny wave, rising and falling against a distant shore.

Like God

One day, the orgasms decide that it's over. Done. *Finis.* They say they are suspending all services. They have been stepped on too often. Looked down on from above. Or worse, taken for granted, forgotten, abandoned. "What happened to the days when we were all you wanted? Thought of? Counted?" they mutter among themselves as they put on their pants and hats, fasten their buttons, and pack their bags. Of course, they have only a handful of belongings, most as light as tissue paper. But even as they slip out of doors and windows in the middle of the night, they are careful not to look back for fear they will burst into tears. After all, they studied you for so long, you are all they dream and know. Like God, they love everything about you. Also like God, they know when you ask, "Was I good?" you don't want the real answer.

The orgasm thinks of writing a spiritual treatise

but then she remembers reading Joseph Campbell's words, "follow your bliss." And how, for so many years, bliss was all she wanted. Bliss and more bliss. Bliss, she thought, was God. She tries not to dwell on bliss these days. She's tired now. But she feels a flash of pleasure just thinking of the word. A small flash, to be sure, but it triggers three other feelings. An *if only* feeling. An *ahhhh* feeling, like a wish she can't fulfill. And greed. She is so sick of greed. In spite of herself, she begins to whine, "Please? Oh, please?" Her *please* sends pangs of longing through her veins, opening her like a door she cannot shut. "Is there no help for an aging orgasm?" she asks. When she's open like that, who knows what will come in? The mornings after, she sighs, "Look what the cat brought in." She always blames the cat.

The Parable of the Burning House

In her last days, the orgasm is like a woman who has just emerged from a burning house. "Who locked all the fire escapes?" she asks. "Who promised us a better life? A better world? The return of Our Lady instead of the endless Amen?" But it's too late. Already, the glaciers are melting. Already, fewer and fewer birds are flying overhead. Everyone turns their backs on her. She sits alone, her scorched limbs folded across her chest. A doctor suggests special ointments for her tender flesh. But they must be applied by you. Only you can save her. Otherwise, she will never heal.

The End

Of course, we were warned. But we never expected it to happen like this. Did anyone know how painful it would be? To soothe the trembling leaves, each one curled inward like a scroll, never to be read again? Such a crazy number of nerves in each, and her small reedy voice, somewhere in the wind, saying, "Hold me! Please!" Did she have a choice? Did we? To caress or not to caress? In this game of life and death, there are so many little griefs. No one prepared us for that last glimpse of her white legs. Her red heels, the only color in the late light.

In Memoriam

Love, I no longer look back
or feel you in the warm breeze
on a summer afternoon.
Nor do I worry how long
you will stay away
or where you've been hiding
all this time.

Nor do I seek you out
or call for you at dusk.
For I am outside the body now
watching the sun set over the water
remembering how we used to play
at this late hour.

Nothing could stop us,
not the neighbors stomping overhead,
not your boss's voice on the answering machine,
not the bill collector banging at the door.
Sometimes, remember? You made me cry.
Other times we screamed and danced,
the radio blaring "Mack the Knife."
And there were those nights we argued,
you drank one Schlitz after another.

Gradually, we grew calm. Or I did.
Yes, calm like an evening prayer,
a ritual at the end of the day.
We held on to one another,
lingering at the entrance of night,
as if we could keep each other
from sinking into that dark lake.

Even in the afterlife

the orgasm remembers you. Of course she does. How you worried you didn't fit in. How you thought you were not one of them. So you sat alone beneath a blue cloak of sky, drawing sunlit plums or ripe peaches in a bowl or something as simple as a silver spoon. As if you could just trace the outlines of love with your pen, even after it had passed. That was once upon a time beneath a blazing sun on the saddest day of an angel's life.

Another Way of Looking at the Orgasm

You and I were one. You and I and the orgasm were three. This, I read, is the true origin of the phrase, "where two or three are gathered in my name, there I am in their midst."

The Afterword,
or Reflections on "The Instruction Manual"

I was reading John Ashbery's poem, "The Instruction Manual" when I wrote "Reflections on the Instruction Manual," only I called it "The Handbook" back then, trying to make it less obvious I was copying Ashbery, whom I love so much. I especially love how he dreamt of writing in Guadalajara, a city with a name like a Mexican dance. Outside of the window in his poem, a band was playing "Scheherazade" by Rimsky-Korsakov, and girls were handing out rose and lemon colored flowers.

When I began writing, I was in Berkeley, California, sitting at a café called The Musical Offering, listening to Mozart sonatas, eating melted brie topped with honey and spring greens on a whole wheat baguette. An Asian girl was sitting at the table across from me, sipping jasmine tea. She was so young and pretty, her hair a river of black silk, I imagined her as one of the flower girls in Ashbery's poem. Instead of a striped dress, she was wearing a T-shirt with the words *Vagina Day* emblazoned in pink letters across her breasts.

Even a vagina has its day in Berkeley, California, I thought. I wondered what a vagina would do on its day. Look for a bite to eat? Shop? Relax with friends? But which friends? I imagined having my own Vagina Day, with poets like Denise Duhamel, Pablo Neruda, Tim Seibles, James Tate, and others, so many others . . .

But I had my doubts. I thought of how old I am now. Days pass when my vagina doesn't want to be bothered anymore. Even the word, vagina, makes me wince. I picture a white room with a nurse and a pair of latex gloves, metal stirrups holding my bare feet, the nurse saying, "This will be just a little pressure." I shudder. I, for one, would never wear a shirt with the words *Vagina Day* on it. A girl has to have a lot of nerve to wear a shirt like that.

But then, as I was ordering a cup of coffee, a whole group of girls entered the café, and I noticed they were all wearing vagina shirts. Some wore vagina sweatshirts and sweatpants, too. Giggling, teasing, and pushing one another, they were a team: Team Vagina girls. They were in such a festive mood, I wished I could join in the fun. I wanted to ask if they thought other words would work in place of vagina.

In her poem "I Knew I'd Sing," Heather McHugh said the word *cunt* has teeth in it. That's why she likes it better than the word *vagina*. Then there's the word *pussy*, with no teeth at all. Pussy, by contrast, is all sweetness and lips. I can easily imagine a pussy that speaks softly and ponders the passing of time. After years of practice, it attains inner peace. Maybe it even levitates. Or looks down at us, as if from above, and dreams. Maybe we are all but a dream of the pussy.

Of a pussy like Guadalajara, the city Ashbery compared to a rose-colored flower. A city that has seen young love, married love, and even aging love. "What next?" Ashbery asks at the end of his poem. "What more is there to do, except stay? And that we cannot do."

He's right, of course. No one stays in a poem forever. Or in a dream of Guadalajara. Even if the vagina had a day, her day would pass. "Alas," I sighed as I turned back to my writing and thought of Ashbery, and how he made me dream. And of all the other poets who have made me dream over the years. I suddenly wanted to write a collection of poems to honor some of the poets I love, a book I tentatively titled *A Handbook of Dreams*, a title I knew I'd change many times as I wrote this book of poems of gratitude, admiration, memories, grief, and love—and also of last orgasms composed by a middle-aged lady who is fanning herself, even now, as she writes these words on a humid summer day in a café called Mystical Omens on the downtown mall in Charlottesville, Virginia.

Notes on the Poems

Many of the poems in this collection are written after poets and artists whose work has inspired me over the years and made my life more beautiful, more magical, more full of meaning.

"Preface" after Lydia Davis, "A Position at the University"

"One Evening, the Orgasm Decides to Give Up on Social Media" after Billy Collins, "Questions about Angels"

"The orgasm thinks people might prefer poodles" after Bertolt Brecht, "If Sharks Were Men"

"The orgasm joins an artist colony" after Robert Hass, "A Story about the Body"

"The Orgasm Fell in Love with Her Writing Professor," after Vassily Kandinsky, *Line, 1934*

"The professor knew she needed help" after Michael Bergt, *Persephone*

"The orgasm reads a book of recipes" after Charles Simic, *The World Doesn't End.*

"Sometimes I feel so inspired" after Ulalume González de León, "Cansiones casi sin palabras"

"If I were a poem" after Maureen Seaton and Denise Duhamel, *Caprice*

"The Orgasm Writes a Short Biography of Nin" after Frank O'Hara, "Autobiographia Literaria"

"Last Night" after Antonio Machado, "Last Night As I Was Sleeping"

"Soul Mate" after Carlos Drummond de Andrade, "The Dirty Hand"

"The Banned Orgasm" after Louise Bourgeois, *Femme Maison*

"My Mother's Advice" after Diego Velázquez, *Rokeby Venus*

"The Visions" after Gian Lorenzo Bernini, *The Ecstasy of Saint Teresa*

"The Accidental Orgasm" after Robert Bly, "The Resemblance Between Your Life and a Dog"

"The Orgasm and Me" after Henri Michaux, "The Statue and Me"

"Her" after Amy Gerstler, "Always"

"The Three Orgasms" after Yannis Ritsos, "The Third One"

"The Shadow of the Orgasm" after James Tate, "The Shadowman"

"The orgasm convinced me I need her after all" after Anne Sexton, "The Starry Night"

"Other People's Orgasms" after Lydia Davis, "Awake in the Night"

"The Bad Orgasm" after Lydia Davis, "The Bad Novel"

"The Orgasm Guard" after Lydia Davis, "The Body Guard"

"The Red Ball" after Michael Bergt, *Red Ball*

"Her Secret" after Alexandros of Antioch, *Venus de Milo*

"Nin and I" after Jorge Louis Borges, "Borges and I"

"I'm a Depressed Orgasm" after David Ignatow, "I'm a Depressed Poem"

"Advice from the Orgasm" after James Tate, "The List of Famous Hats"

"The Letter I Should Have Written to a Young Nin" after Rainer Maria Rilke, *Letters to a Young Poet*

"Not Having an Orgasm" after Mark Halliday, "Non-Tenured"

"What I Keep Telling Nin" after Mary Oliver, "Wild Geese"

"The Curse of the Orgasm" after James Wright, "A Blessing"

"If" after Pablo Neruda, "If You Forget Me"

"Song of the Orgasm" after Walt Whitman, "Song of Myself"

"In the Supermarket of Orgasms" after Allen Ginsberg, "A Supermarket in California" and García Lorca, "The Moon Rising"

"Black Dress on a White Carpet" after César Vallejo, "Black Stone on a White Stone"

"A Simple Fact That Few Really Know" after Günter Kunert, "Daydreams"

"The Orgasm and the Magic Maid" after Franz Kafka, "The Metamorphosis'

"The Orgasm Blues" after Tim Seibles, "Zombie Blues Villanelle"

"Orgasm" after Frank O'Hara, "Why I Am Not a Painter"

"The Innocent Lives of Orgasms" after Mark Strand, "Fictions"

"The Last Orgasm" after Carolyn Forché, "The Colonel"

"Like God" after Günter Kunert, "Attitude Towards a City"

"In Memoriam" after César Vallejo, "To My Brother Miguel in Memoriam"

"Even in the afterlife" after John Ashbery, "A Snowball in Hell"

"The Afterword, or Reflections on 'The Instruction Manual'" after John Ashbery, "The Instruction Manual"

"The Definition of Postmodernism: A Response to Critics of *The Last Orgasm*" after David Lehman, *The Questions of Postmodernism: An Essay*

The Definition of Postmodernism:
A Response to Critics of *The Last Orgasm*

I was in David Lehman's Modern Poetry class when I first heard the term "postmodernism." I remember scribbling in my notes, "The postmodern orgasm is an orgasm having an orgasm having an orgasm." I have no clue what else Dr. Lehman said, or if he even said that, or if I simply wrote that down as one of the many thoughts rushing through my mind. But I imagined it then, the postmodern orgasm, as something I should take into consideration and might write about some day.

Nevertheless, it came as a surprise to me when the critics of *The Last Orgasm* described the book as a postmodern orgasm, or rather, as a collection of postmodern orgasms. "But what," one critic asked, "is a postmodern orgasm?"

Only then did I look up the term. But, as so often happens with all things related to orgasms, the definition varied according to the source.

Wikipedia defined it as "an orgasm of questionable identity or origin."

Webster's defined it as "the orgasm after the orgasm after the orgasm. Also, an ape aping an ape aping an ape aping."

Larousse called it *l'orgasmse post-marché*, or the aftermarket orgasm. Though in Paris, I am told, it is called simply *le post-masqué,* meaning the orgasm without its mask.

The Urban Dictionary defined it as "the orgasm Barbie never had.

Or Tinker Belle. Or Little Miss Muffet, despite the presence of her tuffet."

Cassandra called it "the foreseeable future." Or was that Chicken Little?

On *Fresh Air with Terry Gross*, Red Riding Hood described it as "the pleasure of annihilation."

Deepak Chopra said it is "a natural event of the post-Newtonian universe in which the apple no longer falls from the tree."

Alice Waters, the gourmand, compared it to a winter strawberry. Or "an orgasm recollected in tranquility. Where is the scent of sex?" she asked.

Louise Glück hates both sex and the scent of sex. "How can I be content," she asked, "when there is still that odor in the world?"

Fox News disliked the very idea and blamed the left-wing media.

Anne-Marie Slaughter, the New American feminist, defined it as a part of the *all* that women can't have.

Zeno worried. *To be or almost to be? That is the question of the postmodern orgasm.*

Zeno's detractors argued that that's like the sky asking if it should be blue.

How blue? Which blue? Which hue? the sky wondered, as it grew as white as a sheet of unlined paper and blew away in a gust of wind.

About The Author

Nin Andrews' poems and stories have appeared in many literary journals and anthologies, including *Ploughshares, Agni, The Paris Review*, and four editions of *Best American Poetry*.

The author of seven chapbooks and seven full-length poetry collections, she has won two Ohio Arts Council's individual artist grants, the Pearl Chapbook Contest, the Kent State University chapbook contest, the Gerald Cable Poetry Award, and the Ohioana Prize for poetry. She is also the editor of a book of translations of the Belgian poet Henri Michaux, *Someone Wants to Steal My Name*.

She lives on a farm in Charlottesville, Virginia, with her husband, cows, coyotes, and many bears.

Books from Etruscan Press

Triptych: The Three-Legged World, In Time, and Orpheus & Echo | Peter Grandbois, James McCorkle, and Robert Miltner

The Candle: Poems of Our 20th Century Holocausts | William Heyen

The Confessions of Doc Williams & Other Poems | William Heyen

The Football Corporations | William Heyen

A Poetics of Hiroshima | William Heyen

September 11, 2001: American Writers Respond | Edited by William Heyen

Shoah Train | William Heyen

American Anger: An Evidentiary | H. L. Hix

As Easy As Lying | H. L. Hix

As Much As, If Not More Than | H. L. Hix

Chromatic | H. L. Hix

Demonstrategy: Poetry, For and Against | H. L. Hix

First Fire, Then Birds | H. L. Hix

God Bless | H. L. Hix

I'm Here to Learn to Dream in Your Language | H. L. Hix

Incident Light | H. L. Hix

Legible Heavens | H. L. Hix

Lines of Inquiry | H. L. Hix

Rain Inscription | H. L. Hix

Shadows of Houses | H. L. Hix

Wild and Whirling Words: A Poetic Conversation | Moderated by H. L. Hix

All the Difference | Patricia Horvath

Art Into Life | Frederick R. Karl

Free Concert: New and Selected Poems | Milton Kessler

Who's Afraid of Helen of Troy: An Essay on Love | David Lazar

Parallel Lives | Michael Lind

The Burning House | Paul Lisicky

Museum of Stones | Lynn Lurie

Quick Kills | Lynn Lurie

Synergos | Roberto Manzano

The Gambler's Nephew | Jack Matthews

The Subtle Bodies | James McCorkle

An Archaeology of Yearning | Bruce Mills

Arcadia Road: A Trilogy | Thorpe Moeckel

Venison | Thorpe Moeckel

Etruscan Press Is Proud of Support Received From

Wilkes University

Youngstown State University

The Ohio Arts Council

The Stephen & Jeryl Oristaglio Foundation

The National Endowment for the Arts

The New Mexico Community Foundation

Founded in 2001 with a generous grant from the Oristaglio Foundation, Etruscan Press is a nonprofit cooperative of poets and writers working to produce and promote books that nurture the dialogue among genres, achieve a distinctive voice, and reshape the literary and cultural histories of which we are a part.

etruscan press

www.etruscanpress.org

Etruscan Press books may be ordered from

Consortium Book Sales and Distribution

800.283.3572

www.cbsd.com

Etruscan Press is a 501(c)(3) nonprofit organization.
Contributions to Etruscan Press are tax deductible
as allowed under applicable law.
For more information, a prospectus,
or to order one of our titles,
contact us at books@etruscanpress.org.